FEEL THE BEAT

HIP HOP MUSIC

Tricia Hoffman

Gareth Stevens
PUBLISHING

Please visit our website, www.garethstevens.com. For a free color catalog of all our high-quality books, call toll free 1-800-542-2595 or fax 1-877-542-2596

Cataloging-in-Publication Data

Names: Hoffman, Tricia.
Title: Hip-hop music / Tricia Hoffman.
Description: Buffalo, NY : Gareth Stevens Publishing, 2027. | Series: Feel the beat | Includes glossary and index.
Identifiers: ISBN 9781482480573 (pbk.) | ISBN 9781482480580 (library bound) | ISBN 9781482480597 (ebook)
Subjects: LCSH: Rap (Music)--History and criticism--Juvenile literature. | Hip-hop--History--Juvenile literature.
Classification: LCC ML3531.H644 2027 | DDC 781.649--dc23

First Edition

Published in 2027 by
Gareth Stevens Publishing
2544 Clinton Street
Buffalo, NY 14224

Designer: Kathy Walsh/Beeline Media & Design, Inc.
Editor: Tricia Hoffman

Photo credits: Cover, Maxim Blinkov/Shutterstock.com; cover, pp. 1–24 (music note background) Gaianami Design/Shutterstock.com; p 4 Artie Medvedev/Shutterstock.com; p 7 @Wiki/Wiki; p 8 Nomad_ Soul/Shutterstock.com; p 9 A_Lesik, hurricanehank/Shutterstock.com; p 10 Featureflash Photo Agency/ Shutterstock.com; p 11 DFP Photographic, lev radin/Shutterstock.com; p 12 Lanang Banget/Shutterstock. com; p 13 Anton_Ivanov, Michael A Walker Jr, A_Lesik/Shutterstock.com; p 14 Jgphotographydetroit/ Shutterstock.com; p 15 Franklin Sheard Jr, L Paul Mann/Shutterstock.com; p 16 Tik.tak/Shutterstock.com; p 18 hurricanehank/Shutterstock.com; p 19 oneinchpunch/Shutterstock.com; p 20 Christian Bertrand/ Shutterstock.com; p 21 Jgphotographydetroit/Shutterstock.com; p 23 A_Lesik, Jamie Lamor Thompson, Markus Wissmann, Ben Houdijk/Shutterstock.com; p 24 jgphotographydetroit/Shutterstock.com; p 25 Kaspars Grinvalds, Xavier Lorenzo/Shutterstock.com; p 26 chaossart/Shutterstock.com; p 27 Here Now/ Shutterstock.com; p 28 Featureflash Photo Agency/Shutterstock.com; p 29 Nikola Spasenoski/@Wiki

Printed in China

CPSIA compliance information: Batch #QS27GS: For further information contact Gareth Stevens, New York, New York at 1-800-542-2595.

Table of Contents

Music for Everyone

Some people say that hip hop music speaks for everyone. It helps young people share their thoughts through music. It brings people together.

Hip hop is one of the most popular types of music in the world. People love this **genre** because it has strong **beats**. The words rhyme and sound good together.

Hip hop artists talk about their lives and dreams. They talk about their communities. They use their voices to make cool sounds.

Get ready to explore the world of hip hop!

The Birth of Hip Hop Music

Hip hop music started in New York City in the 1970s. Many neighborhoods in New York were having hard times. People did not have much money. But they had creativity and music.

DJ Kool Herc played music at a back-to-school party for teens. He used two **turntables**. He noticed that some parts of songs made people dance more. These parts had strong beats. He played these parts again and again to keep people dancing. From there, hip hop was born.

DJ Kool Herc

THE FATHER OF HIP HOP

DJ Kool Herc, whose real name is Clive Campbell, is considered the founding father of hip hop. He was born in Jamaica and moved to New York at age 12. "Herc" is short for "Hercules."

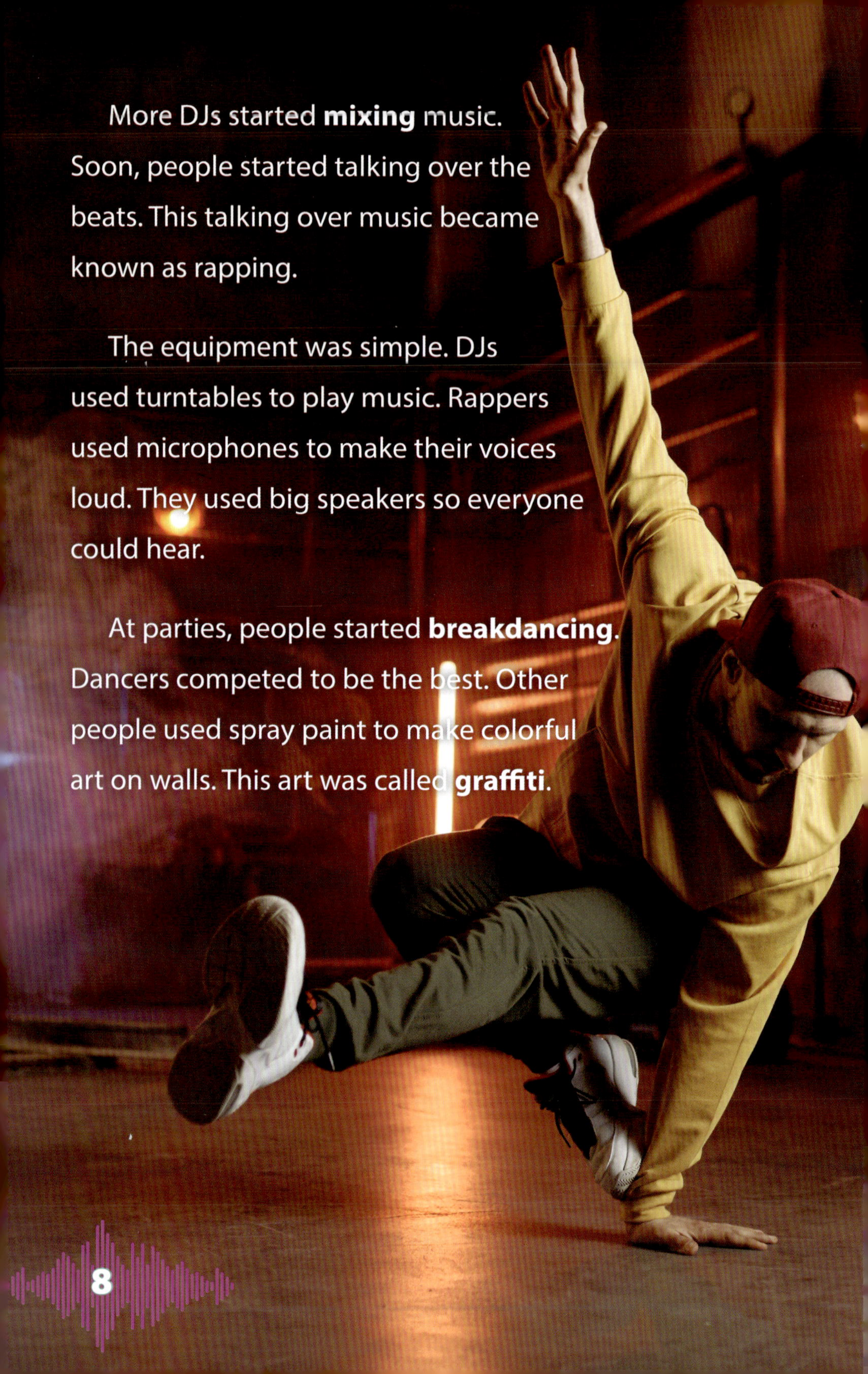

More DJs started **mixing** music. Soon, people started talking over the beats. This talking over music became known as rapping.

The equipment was simple. DJs used turntables to play music. Rappers used microphones to make their voices loud. They used big speakers so everyone could hear.

At parties, people started **breakdancing**. Dancers competed to be the best. Other people used spray paint to make colorful art on walls. This art was called **graffiti**.

HIP HOP CULTURE

There are four main parts of hip hop: DJing, rapping, breakdancing, and graffiti art. All four parts come together to create hip hop culture. The music is just one part of something much bigger.

Hip Hop Music Throughout the Years

In the 1980s, hip hop music got bigger. New artists like Run-DMC and LL Cool J became famous. Hip hop music videos played on TV. More people learned about hip hop this way.

Hip hop artists also started using new technology. They used drum machines to make beats. These machines could repeat the same drum sound again and again. They also used **samplers**. Samplers could take pieces of old songs and use them in new ways.

Run-DMC

LL Cool J

Sugarhill Gang

HIP HOP TAKES OFF

The first hip hop song to become famous was "Rapper's Delight" by the Sugarhill Gang in 1979.

The 1980s and 1990s were called the "Golden Age of Hip Hop." Many people think this was the best time for hip hop music. Artists like Tupac, The Notorious B.I.G., and Nas made songs that people still love today. The music became more complex. The **lyrics** became deeper and more meaningful.

Hip hop music split into different styles during this time. Some hip hop was hard and loud. Some was more calm. East Coast hip hop sounded different from West Coast hip hop. Each region had its own style.

Tupac

statue of The Notorious B.I.G.

Nas

In the 2000s, artists like Eminem, 50 Cent, and OutKast sold millions of **records**. Hip hop songs played on every radio station. Music videos had big budgets and looked like movies.

Today, hip hop is still growing and changing. New artists use computers to make beats. They share their music on the internet. Some hip hop songs mix singing with rapping. Hip hop keeps finding new ways to surprise and excite fans.

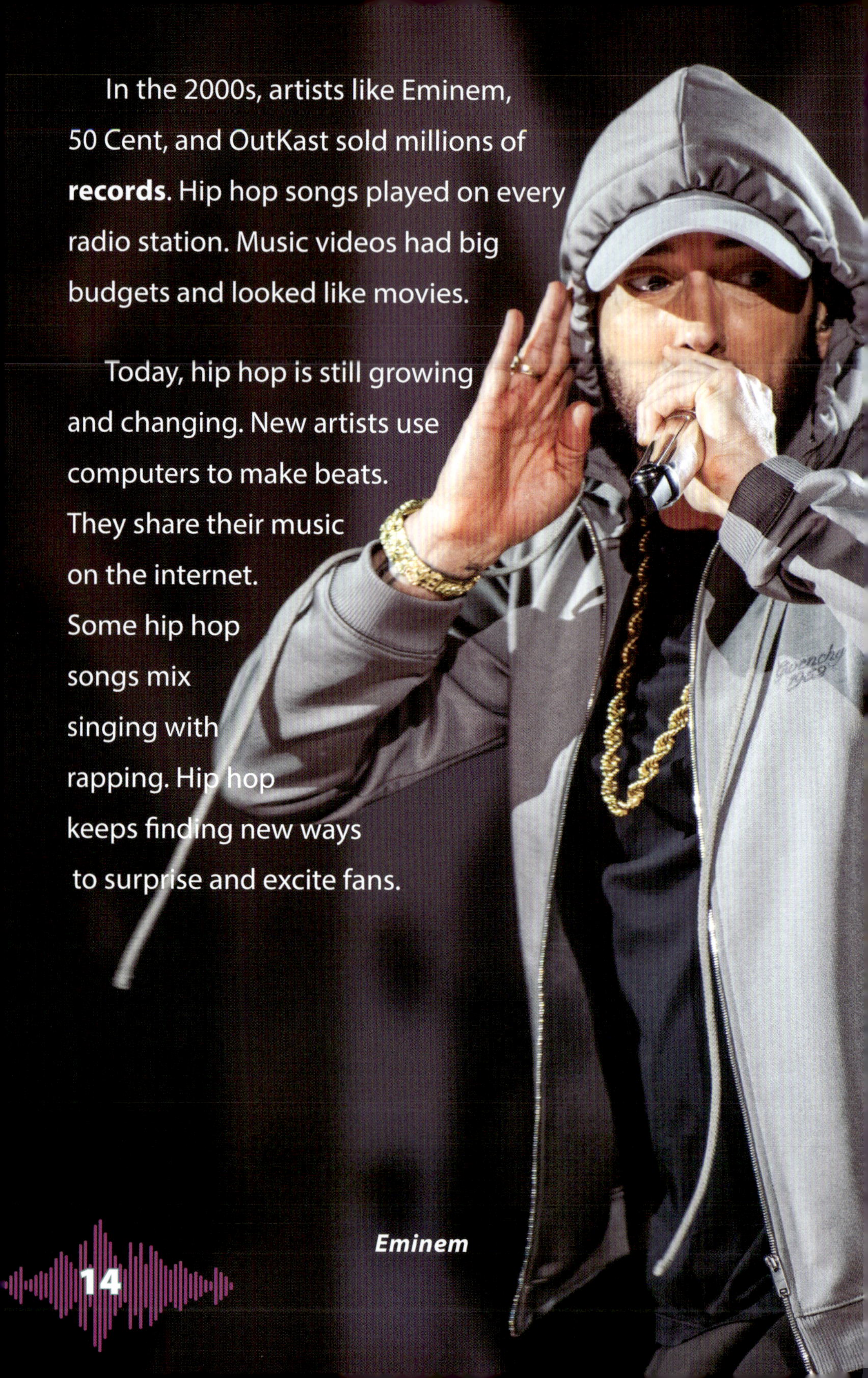

Eminem

50 Cent

Wu-Tang Clan

THE MOST EXPENSIVE ALBUM

The Wu-Tang Clan made only one copy of their album, *Once Upon a Time in Shaolin*. It sold for $2 million in 2015. Only one person in the world owns it!

What Makes Music "Hip Hop"?

What makes a song hip hop? There are several things that make hip hop special.

The most important part of hip hop is the beat. Hip hop beats are strong and steady. They usually have four beats that repeat. The beats often come from drum machines or computers. Sometimes producers take drum sounds from old songs and loop them. This means they play the same few seconds again and again.

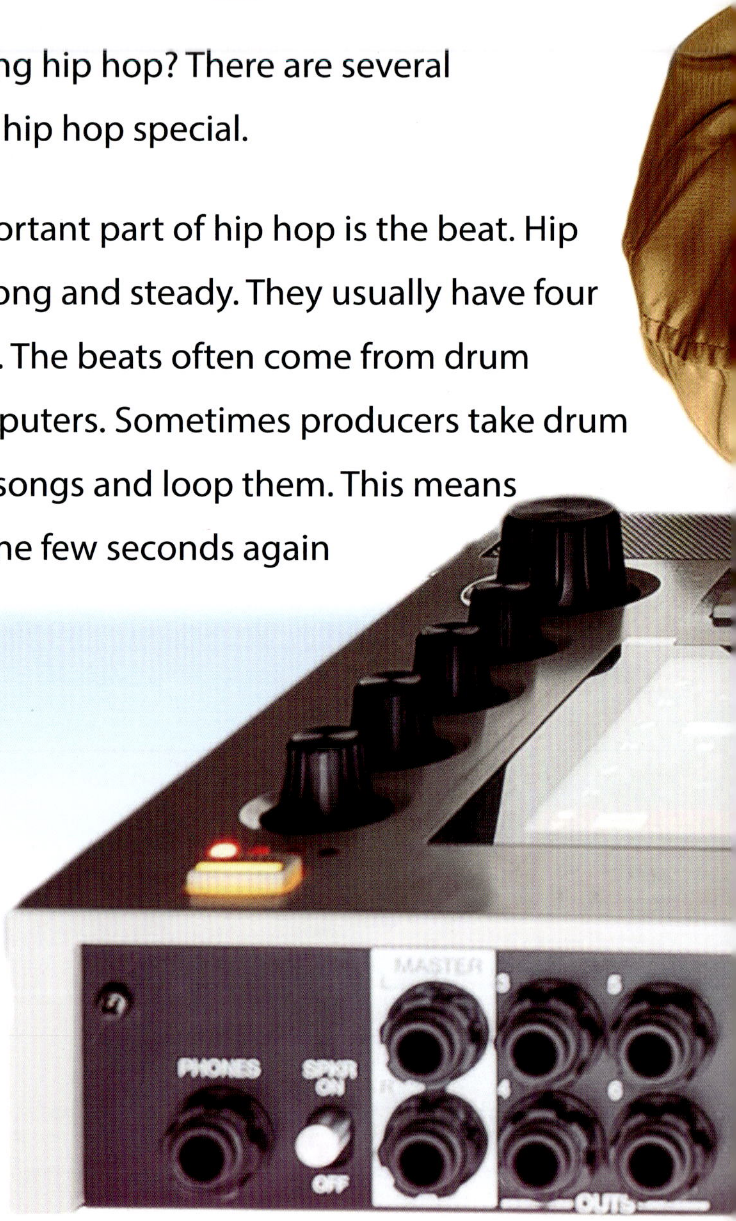

PHONO
IN
SD CARD
CV/GATE
MIDI OUT

Hip hop also uses sampling. Sampling means taking pieces of other songs and using them in new hip hop songs. A hip hop artist might take a guitar sound from an old rock song. Or they might use the horn section from a jazz record. They mix these sounds with new beats and rap to create something fresh.

The bass is very important in hip hop too. The bass makes low, deep sounds that you can feel in your chest. Hip hop songs usually have strong bass lines that help drive the beat.

Another big part of hip hop is rapping. Rapping is like talking, but with rhythm and rhyme. Rappers match their words to the beat of the music. Good rappers can rap fast or slow. They can make their voices sound different for different songs.

Hip hop lyrics often tell stories. Rappers might talk about their childhoods. They might rap about their dreams or their problems. Some hip hop songs are funny. Others are serious and make people think about important topics.

Many hip hop songs also have a **hook** or chorus. This is a catchy part that repeats during the song. This helps people remember the words and sing along.

Eminem

QUICK TALKING!

Eminem is one of the fastest rappers of all time. He currently holds the world record for rapping 225 words in just 30 seconds. That's almost eight words each second!

Hip Hop Music Around the World

People make hip hop music around the world. They use their own language, their own instruments, and talk about their own lives.

Germany has one of the biggest hip hop scenes in Europe. German rappers like Cro rap about life in German cities. He wears a panda mask when he performs!

In Japan, rap groups sometimes mix traditional Japanese instruments with modern hip hop beats.

South African artists like Sho Madjozi and Nasty C rap in languages like Xitsonga and Zulu. They mix hip hop with traditional African music. West African countries like Senegal and Ghana also have strong hip hop cultures.

Cro

Sho Madjozi

Nasty C

Hip Hop Music Today and Tomorrow

Hip hop music today is more popular than ever. Artists like Kendrick Lamar, Travis Scott, and Doja Cat are some of the biggest stars in the world. Their songs get billions of plays on music apps.

Technology has changed how hip hop music is made. Today, anyone with a computer can make hip hop beats. There are apps that let people create and share music anywhere.

Kendrick Lamar

Artists use social media to connect with fans. Sometimes, a 15-second clip on TikTok can make a song famous around the world. Fans can discover new artists every day!

A STRONG MESSAGE

Experts say that hip hop can make young people feel powerful. In schools, teachers use hip hop to help students learn. This makes learning fun and helps students remember what they study.

What will hip hop sound like in the future? New technology might help create new sounds. Artists might use artificial intelligence to help write songs. Virtual reality might let fans feel like they are right next to their favorite rappers during concerts.

One thing is certain—hip hop will keep growing and changing. New artists will find fresh ways to express themselves.

Hip hop started in New York City. Now, it is a global language that connects millions of people from all over the world.

HOME OF
HIPHOP

Hip Hop Music Superstars

Hip hop music is loved all over the world. Some of these artists were the first to try new ways of making music, and others have won big awards for their songs. These hip hop superstars show us how this type of music grew from something small to something huge that people everywhere enjoy.

Grandmaster Flash
1970s-1980s

Grandmaster Flash is often called "The Father of Hip Hop." He was one of the first DJs to use turntables to make new sounds. He created a way to mix songs together without stopping the music. His group made the famous song "The Message" in the early 1980s.

Run-DMC
1980s-1990s

Run-DMC was the first hip hop group to have a gold album—that means it sold more than 500,000 copies! They made hip hop music popular on MTV. They wore black leather jackets and Adidas shoes without laces. Their style became a fashion symbol of the 1980s.

Tupac Shakur
1990s

Tupac was one of the most famous rappers ever. He sold more than 75 million records around the world. Tupac wrote songs about important things like helping poor people and stopping violence. Even though he died at age 25, he continues to influence hip hop music today.

Missy Elliott
1990s-today

Missy Elliott is known for her creative music videos and fun songs. She was the first female rapper to win five Grammy Awards! She writes and produces music for many other famous singers. She is known for being kind and helping other artists succeed.

Eminem
1990s-today

Eminem is one of the best-selling music artists of all time. He got his big break in 1997 when he won second place in the Rap Olympics. Since then, he has sold more than 220 million records! He also made a movie about his life called *8 Mile*.

Kendrick Lamar
2010s-today

Kendrick Lamar is known for writing songs with important messages. He won a Pulitzer Prize for his music. He is the first rapper ever to win this award! He grew up in California and writes about his neighborhood. Many people think he is one of the best rappers alive today.

Glossary

beats (beets): the steady rhythm that repeats throughout a hip hop song

breakdancing (BRAYK-dan-sing): a style of dancing with quick moves and spins that started with hip hop culture

DJ (DEE-jay): a person who plays and mixes recorded music for an audience

genre (ZHAHN-ruh): a type or kind of music, like hip hop, rock, or pop

hook (huk): a catchy part of a song that repeats and is easy to remember

lyrics (LIR-iks): the words of a song that tell the story

mixing (miks-ing): combining two or more songs to create a continuous sound

records (REK-urdz): flat, round discs that music is stored on so people can buy it and play it at home

samplers (SAMP-lurz): special machines that can take sounds from old songs so that they can be used in new songs

turntables (TURN-tay-buhlz): equipment that DJs use to play records and mix music

Fact Check

1. Where did hip hop music start?
   a. New York City b. Los Angeles c. Chicago
2. What is rapping?
   a. dancing to music
   b. talking over beats with rhyme
   c. playing drums
3. What do samplers do?
   a. make voices louder
   b. take pieces of old songs for new songs
   c. play records

Answers: 1. a, 2. b, 3. b

On the Internet

100 Greatest Hip-Hop Songs of All Time
www.rollingstone.com/music/music-lists/100-greatest-hip-hop-songs-of-all-time-105784/
What makes a hip hop song great? Read interesting details about some of the most famous hip hop songs in history.

Hip Hop
https://kids.britannica.com/kids/article/hip-hop/399968
Get an overview of the world of hip hop with Britannica Kids.

Publisher's note to educators and parents: Our editors have carefully reviewed these websites to ensure that they are suitable for students. Many websites change frequently, however, and we cannot guarantee that a site's future contents will continue to meet our high standards of quality and educational value. Be advised that students should be closely supervised whenever they access the internet.

Index

About the Author

Tricia Hoffman is a writer, editor, reader, and runner. She lives in Columbus, Ohio, with her husband and two sons. She started listening to Eminem as a teenager and still loves his music to this day. She enjoys music of all kinds and loves to sing along.